I0217891

KIDS

BOOK OF

WHY?

MEKO

Copyright © 2020 Meko
All rights reserved.

ISBN: 978-0-578-65869-8
Library of Congress Control
Number: 2020905217
Eagle Life
Publications, Dallas, TX

ASK BIRDIE...

WHY DO WE HAVE TO GO TO THE DOCTOR?

- Going to the <u>DOCTOR</u> can help us feel better when we get sick!

- Going to the <u>DOCTOR</u> can help to stop us from getting sick!

- If we go to the <u>DOCTOR</u>, it can help us to live longer!

- Some <u>DOCTORS</u> are fun because they give us toys and treats to help us feel better!

ASK BIRDIE...

WHY DO WE NEED TREES?

- <u>TREES</u> are the biggest plants on the planet, they help us with everything we need to stay alive!

- <u>TREES</u> gives us oxygen, purify the air, helps our water cycle, trees helps with climate change, wood, food, and more!

- <u>TREES</u> can give us medicine for when we get sick!

- <u>TREES</u> helps to protect wildlife and other animals!

ASK BIRDIE...

WHY CAN'T ANIMALS TALK?

- **ANIMALS** have their own ways to communicate with each other!

- **ANIMALS** chest, throats, and mouths are made differently than humans!

- Some **BIRDS** can hear sounds and learn how to make that sound and repeat it! They can sound like humans, machines, and even vehicles!

- **ANIMALS** learn and communicate differently, but they are smart!

ASK BIRDIE...

WHY SHOULD WE TAKE A BATH EVERYDAY?

- Taking a **BATH** keeps us clean so that we will not stink!

- Taking a **BATH** takes away dead skin and bacteria!

- We don't have to take a **BATH** everyday because it can make our skin dry and take away good skin oils, but a lot of people take a shower or bath everyday to feel clean!

- **BATHING** can help our heart, it can help us to breathe easier, it can also help our brain and muscles!

ASK BIRDIE...

WHY ARE STARS IN THE SKY?

- All <u>STARS</u> except the sun appear in the sky as shining points at night! The sun is also a star, and it is close enough to the Earth to give us daylight!

- <u>STARS</u> have a lot of energy that keeps the sun hot and shining bright in the sky!

- <u>STARS</u> in the sky helped ancient explorers navigate the seas, and now they help modern-day scientists to navigate the universe!

- <u>STARS</u> are in the sky because they are balls of gas held together by its own gravity!

ASK BIRDIE...

WHY SHOULD WE EAT A LOT OF VEGETABLES?

- <u>VEGETABLES</u> makes us stronger! Especially leafy green vegetables!

- <u>VEGETABLES</u> makes us smarter!

- <u>VEGETABLES</u> helps us to run faster!

- <u>VEGETABLES</u> helps us to grow healthier!

ASK BIRDIE...

WHY DO AIRPLANES FLY?

- <u>AIRPLANES</u> fly because they are able to create a force called Lift, which normally moves the plane upward.

- <u>AIRPLANES</u> fly because it can carry a lot of people at one time!

- Flying on an <u>AIRPLANE</u> is safer than riding in a car!

- <u>AIRPLANES</u> fly to take us places faster!

- <u>AIRPLANES</u> fly because people enjoy watching airplanes fly!

ASK BIRDIE...

WHY SHOULD WE READ BOOKS?

- READING helps us to learn more!

- READING is healthy for our brains, it helps us to think better!

- READING can be fun!

- READING makes us smarter!

- READING can make us happy, and it can help our memory!

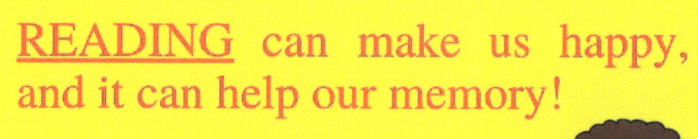

ASK BIRDIE...

WHY CAN'T BABIES WALK?

- <u>BABIES</u> brains have a lot to learn, so they have to learn how to control their body movements first!

- <u>BABIES</u> have to eat, drink, and sleep a lot so that their bodies can grow!

- <u>BABIES</u> can crawl when they get a little bigger and stronger!

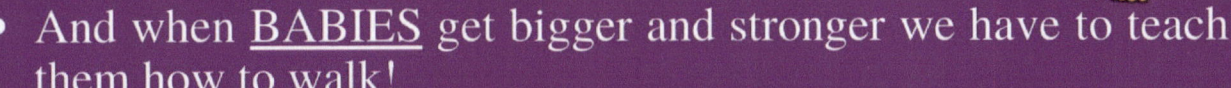

- And when <u>BABIES</u> get bigger and stronger we have to teach them how to walk!

WHY DO WE HAVE A BELLY BUTTON?

- Because when we were in our mommy's belly, a cord grew to help us to stay alive inside of her belly!

ASK BIRDIE...

- After we are born, the cord is cut and our belly button marks the spot of our universe! It's also called a <u>NAVEL</u>!

- Our belly buttons has friendly bacteria that helps us by competing with, and attacking viruses and germs that land on our skin!

- I call it my love button from mommy since birth!

WHY SHOULD WE BRUSH OUR TEETH?

ASK BIRDIE...

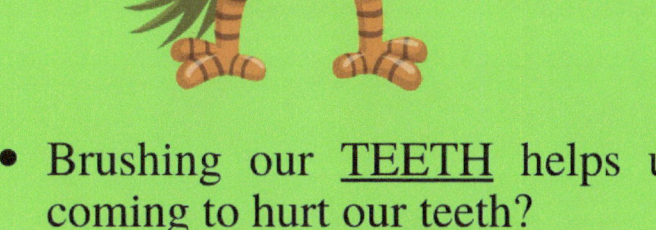

- Brushing our <u>TEETH</u> helps us to keep our teeth strong!

- Brushing our <u>TEETH</u> helps us to not get sick because of dirty gums!

- Brushing our <u>TEETH</u> helps us to eat food without pain coming to hurt our teeth?

- Brushing our <u>TEETH</u> helps to keep our teeth white and our breath fresh!

WHY DO SEEDS GROW?

ASK BIRDIE...

- <u>SEEDS</u> grow and produce good food for people to eat!

- <u>SEEDS</u> grow to help feed animals!

- <u>SEEDS</u> grow to give us beautiful flowers!

- <u>SEEDS</u> grow to give us medicine for when we get sick!

ASK BIRDIE...

WHY ARE PEOPLE DIFFERENT COLORS?

- People are different colors because of melanin! Our <u>SKIN</u> can be very pale to very dark, some people make more melanin than others, that's why people are different colors!

- Melanin creates the color of our <u>SKIN</u>, eyes, and hair color!

- People can be different colors because of the sun, the sun can make your <u>SKIN</u> look different!

- It is fun being different colors, and being friends with people of different colors!

WHY DO SOME PEOPLE HAVE CURLY HAIR?

ASK BIRDIE...

- Some parents have curly <u>HAIR</u>, so their child has curly hair!

- Some <u>HAIR</u> is curly by the shape of the follicles that's in our head!

- Some <u>HAIR</u> is curly when it gets wet, it's curly because it's our naturally good hair that's made to be curly!

- Some <u>HAIR</u> is curly because it looks good curly!

WHY DOES IT SNOW?

ASK BIRDIE...

- It <u>SNOWS</u> because tiny ice crystals in the clouds stick together and gets heavy enough to fall to the ground!

- It <u>SNOWS</u> because snowflakes form when water freeze into ice in the cold clouds!

- <u>SNOW</u> is an important part of the Earth's climate system, snow helps to regulate the temperature of the Earth's surface! And when the snow melts, the water helps to fill rivers!

- It <u>SNOWS</u> for a lot of reasons, but my favorite is because it can be fun to watch the snow fall, and play in it! We can even build a snowman!

WHY SHOULD WE WASH OUR HANDS?

ASK BIRDIE...

- A lot of bad things can spread around to everyone if we don't <u>WASH</u> our hands with soap and clean running water!

 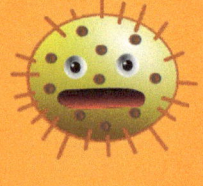 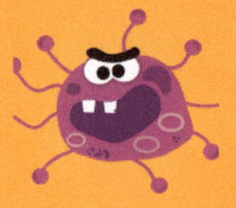

- <u>WASHING</u> our hands can help with stopping us from getting sick!

- We can stay alive longer if we <u>WASH</u> our hands!

- It can be fun singing the alphabet song or singing the happy birthday song while <u>WASHING</u> our hands!

WHY IS FIRE HOT?

ASK BIRDIE...

- <u>FIRE</u> is hot because thermal energy (heat) is released from chemicals!

- The chemicals turn fuel and oxygen into carbon dioxide and water that releases energy that is visible as <u>FLAMES</u>!

- Fuel + Oxygen + Energy + Carbon Dioxide + Water + more Energy = <u>HOT</u> gases!

- <u>FIRE</u> is hot because the energy stored in fuel is released really fast!

WHY DO WE NEED SLEEP?

ASK BIRDIE...

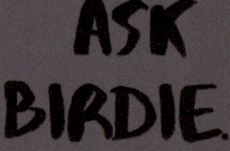

- We need <u>SLEEP</u> because it helps us to restore our bodies!

- <u>SLEEPING</u> helps our memory!

- <u>SLEEPING</u> helps us to stay healthy and feeling our best!

 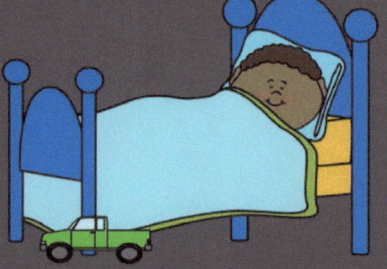

- We can not survive without <u>SLEEP</u>, no one can live long without going to sleep!

WHY DO BEES MAKE HONEY?

ASK BIRDIE...

- Honey <u>BEES</u> make honey to store food to eat over the winter!

- Not all <u>BEES</u> make honey, but honey bees, especially female bees! Buzz around from flower to flower, while they also build and defend the hive and take care of the Queen! But if they don't have enough honey to survive, the entire colony dies!

- Honey <u>BEES</u> make honey because it's full of nutrients, and is a great energy food!

- Pure honey can last forever!

WHY DO WE HAVE TO GO TO SCHOOL?

ASK BIRDIE...

- We have to go to <u>SCHOOL</u> to gain the skills and education that we need to live a successful life!

- <u>SCHOOL</u> teaches us social skills that we need to communicate with people!

- <u>SCHOOL</u> helps us to be smarter and to grow with friends!

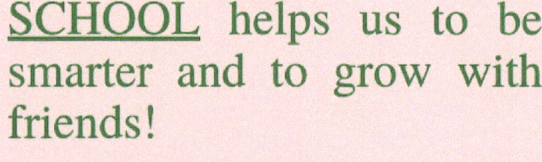

- <u>SCHOOL</u> is important because we learn how to read, write, and do math! We learn about people, places, and nature!

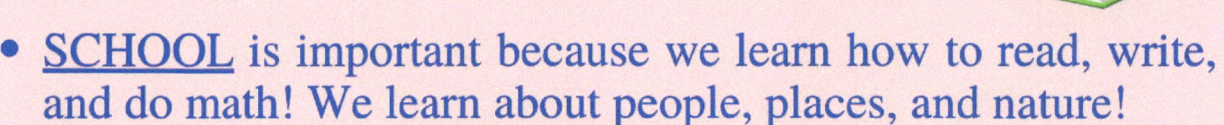

WHY SHOULD WE BE NICE TO PEOPLE?

ASK BIRDIE...

- We should be <u>NICE</u> because being mean isn't fun!

- Being <u>NICE</u> helps to improve our relationships and our health!

- Being <u>NICE</u> helps our mind!

Be Kind

- Being <u>NICE</u> can help us to live longer!

- Being <u>NICE</u> can help us to make new friends, and it can make us and other people happy!

WHY DOES IT RAIN?

ASK BIRDIE...

- It <u>RAINS</u> because we all need water to stay alive!

- It <u>RAINS</u> because plants need water to stay alive!

- Clouds have tiny water drops in it, and when the drops join together they get heavy and fall from the clouds as <u>RAIN</u>!

- It <u>RAINS</u> because warm air turns the water from the rivers, lakes, and oceans into vapor that goes into the air!

WHY DO WE COUGH?

ASK BIRDIE...

- COUGHING helps us to get rid of bad things in our bodies!

- COUGHING can mean that we are getting sick and may need medicine to feel better!

- COUGHING is a normal healthy function of our bodies!

- If germs, dust, or anything irritate our throat and airway, our bodies automatically responds because COUGHING helps to protect our bodies! Just like sneezing or blinking helps us!

WHY SHOULD WE FOLLOW RULES?

ASK BIRDIE...

- We follow <u>RULES</u> because it keeps everyone safe!

- <u>RULES</u> can help everyone to have more fun in life!

- <u>RULES</u> can stop bad things from happening to us!

- Following <u>RULES</u> can help us to be better and smarter!

WHY DO WE HAVE RAINBOWS?

ASK BIRDIE...

- We have <u>RAINBOWS</u> when the sun is behind us and falling rain is in front of us!

- We see <u>RAINBOWS</u> when a reflection of light in water droplets makes light appear in the sky that forms a multicolored circular arc!

- When the sunlight appears in the section of the sky directly opposite of the sun, it causes a <u>RAINBOW</u>!

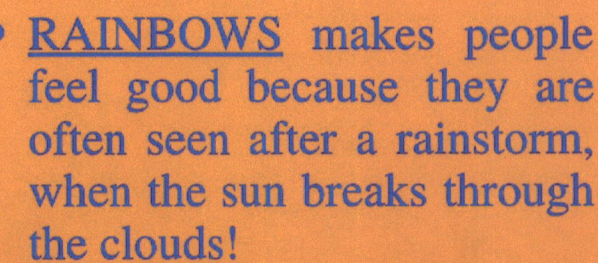

- <u>RAINBOWS</u> makes people feel good because they are often seen after a rainstorm, when the sun breaks through the clouds!

WHY SHOULD WE DRINK A LOT OF WATER?

ASK BIRDIE...

- WATER is good for our skin!

- WATER can give us energy!

- WATER helps our muscles and our brain!

 Our bodies and blood is made of a lot of WATER, so we need to drink a lot of WATER to stay strong and healthy!

WHY ARE NUTS HEALTHY TO EAT?

ASK BIRDIE...

- <u>NUTS</u> helps to keep our hearts strong and healthy!

- If you are allowed to eat <u>NUTS</u>, nuts can help us to stay alive longer!

- <u>NUTS</u> helps our bodies to fight against getting sick with diseases like cancer, diabetes, and more!

- <u>NUTS</u> can help our skin, our bones, our organs, and our muscles to stay strong!

WHY DOES THE WIND BLOW?

ASK BIRDIE...

- The <u>WIND</u> blows because of the difference in the air pressure!

- The air moves from high to low pressure that makes the <u>WIND</u> come in fast and slow!

- The <u>WIND</u> is from the Earth spinning itself!

- If the <u>WIND</u> stops blowing then it will mess up the Earth and atmosphere!

SMART
&
EARLY
LEARNING

For more information about
Meko's
Smart & Early Learning initiative,
visit
www.eaglelifepublications.net